LESVOS

TRAVEL GUIDE 2024-2025

Your Passport to Exploring Lesvos's Hidden Treasures and Scenic Wonders in 2024-2025

Jimmy Britt

COPYRIGHT © 2024 BY JIMMY BRITT

TABLE OF CONTENTS

CHAPTER ONE: INTRODUCTION TO LESVOS

Greece's beautiful island of Lesvos, usually referred to as Lesbos, is situated in the northeastern Aegean Sea. Sought after for its pristine beauty, historical importance, and many cultural offerings, the island has long been a center of human endeavors. Lesvos draws tourists looking for a true Greek experience because of its distinctive combination of serene beaches, charming towns, and lush terrain. The island's other major exports include fine olive oil and ouzo, the distinctive anise-flavored liquor of Greece, which have greatly influenced the country's culture. To appreciate the island's allure and history, let's examine its topography, climate, history, and culture.

History and Cultural Overview

Ancient and Legendary Origins

Lesvos has an extensive history spanning millennia, and its legendary associations are profoundly ingrained in Greek folklore. The deity of wine, fertility, and celebration, Dionysus, was said to have been born on the island. In antiquity, the capital of the island, Mytilene, was a significant hub for learning and culture. Lesvos may have been inhabited as early as the Bronze Age, or about the third millennium BCE, according to archaeological findings. Because of its advantageous position, the island played a major role in the Aegean trade routes.

Lesvos was renowned in antiquity for its poets and thinkers. The poet Sappho, who flourished in the seventh century BCE, is perhaps the most famous person connected to the island. Sappho was one of the most respected authors of antiquity because of her lyric poetry, which centered on love and introspection. Though mostly disjointed, her writings have influenced poets and authors throughout history, elevating her to the status of a figure of ardor and inventiveness.

Other well-known individuals from Lesvos include the philosopher Theophrastus, a pupil of Aristotle and the father of botanical science, and the poet Alcaeus. These thinkers helped the island gain its reputation as a hub of creativity and ideas in antiquity. Renowned for its public institutions and architecture, the ancient city of Mytilene flourished as a cultural center that drew philosophers, authors, and politicians from all across the Greek world.

Ottoman and Byzantine Periods

Lesvos was conquered by many empires after the fall of Greek civilization. The island remained a significant hub for trade and culture during the Roman and Byzantine eras. Christianity began to expand across Lesvos during this period, and several churches and monasteries were constructed—some of which are still standing today. Established in the sixteenth century, the Monastery of Limonos continues to be a significant place of worship and a reminder of the island's Byzantine history.

Lesvos was ruled by the Genoese in the late medieval era starting in 1355, and the Gattelusi dynasty ruled the island for more than a century. Lesvos, however, was taken over by the Ottomans in 1462, and so began more than 400 years of Ottoman domination. Lesvos had a blending of Greek and Ottoman influences throughout this period, which was evident in its cuisine, architecture, and cultural customs. Greek Orthodox churches were constructed beside mosques and Turkish baths, resulting in a setting with a rich diversity of cultures.

Lesvos was conquered by the Ottomans in the early 20th century and freed in 1912 during the First Balkan War. With the signing of the Treaty of

Lausanne in 1923, the island was included in contemporary Greece.

From the 20th Century to the Present

The population exchange between Greece and Turkey in the early 20th century had a significant impact on Lesvos, as thousands of ethnic Greek immigrants from Asia Minor added to the island's population and culture. The manufacturing of olive oil was one of the principal industries, and agriculture remained the main driver of the island's economy.

Lesvos's involvement in the refugee problem has brought it international recognition in recent decades. The island has played a leading role in the reception of refugees and migrants from Middle Eastern crisis zones, especially at the height of the Syrian civil war in the mid-2010s. The island's recent history has been affected by this humanitarian crisis, which has brought together

8

local communities and foreign relief agencies to give help.

Lesvos continues to be a representation of tenacity and cultural pride in spite of these difficulties. Its history, spanning from antiquity to the present, demonstrates its continuing significance as a hub for human compassion, education, and culture.

Geography and Climate of Lesvos

Overview of Geography

Lesvos, spanning an estimated 1,630 square kilometers (630 square miles), is the third biggest island in Greece. Situated on Turkey's coast in the northeastern Aegean Sea, it is divided by the narrow Mytilini Strait. Due to its closeness to Asia Minor, it has long been a hub for migration, commerce, and culture.

The island's varied terrain offers a breathtaking variety of environments, ranging from rough mountain ranges to lush, fertile plains. Mount Lepetymnos (968 meters) in the north and Mount Olympus (967 meters) in the island's center are the two main volcanic mountain ranges that dominate Lesvos. The island's diverse geography is influenced by these mountains, which provide striking vistas and microclimate.

The Gulf of Kalloni, an inland sea in Lesvos' southern region, is one of the island's most distinctive geological characteristics. This broad, shallow gulf serves as a significant migratory bird stopover and is home to a diverse range of organisms. The marshes that round the Gulf of Kalloni are a favorite spot for nature enthusiasts and birdwatchers since they are home to several bird species, including flamingos.

Because Lesvos is a volcanic island, it is also home to a number of hot springs. Since ancient times, people have utilized these thermal springs, which are situated in areas like Eftalou and Polichnitos, for medicinal reasons. The island's long history of agricultural and wellness tourism may be attributed to its wealth of natural resources, which include mineral-rich waters and fertile soil.

Lesvos's climate

The Mediterranean climate that Lesvos experiences is characterized by hot, dry summers and warm, rainy winters. The island has a somewhat distinct climate from other Greek islands due to its position in the northeastern Aegean, with higher variance in temperature and precipitation.

On Lesvos, summers are usually sunny and pleasant, with average highs of 25–30°C (77–86°F). The warmest months of the year are July and August, when sporadic heatwaves raise the temperature to 35°C (95°F). Nonetheless, the island benefits from mild breezes due to its hilly topography and closeness to the sea, especially in coastal regions and higher elevations.

The island receives a lot of sunlight and little rainfall in the summer, which makes it a great place for beachgoers and outdoor lovers. Swimming, sailing, and other water sports are popular in Lesvos because of the spotless sky and warm Aegean seas.

Lesvos has milder but wetter winters with average highs of 10°C to 15°C (50°F to 59°F). Although it doesn't often snow on the island, during really cold periods, snow may sometimes fall at higher altitudes in the highlands. The wettest months on the island are December and January, with the majority of the yearly rainfall falling between November and March. The island's luxuriant vegetation, which includes its well-known olive groves, is maintained by the winter showers.

The transitional seasons of spring and autumn are among the greatest times to visit Lesvos. There are few visitors and nice weather at certain times of the year. The island is especially lovely in the spring, when the olive trees are in full bloom and the landscape is blanketed with wildflowers. These seasons see a boom in bird migration, drawing in naturalists and ornithologists both.

In summary

Lesvos is an island with exceptional natural beauty, an extensive past, and a distinct cultural legacy. Lesvos has maintained its importance throughout the ages, from its beginnings as a hub of Greek scholarship and art to its involvement in the current refugee crisis. Together with its Mediterranean temperature, the island's varied landscapes—which include tranquil beaches, volcanic mountains, and lush plains—make it the perfect place for visitors looking to combine exploration, leisure, and cultural immersion. Lesvos provides a classic Greek experience that is enriching and memorable, whether you are sipping a drink of ouzo by the sea, strolling through the historic alleys of Mytilene, or taking a thermal bath.

CHAPTER TWO: GETTING TO LESVOS AND PRACTICAL INFORMATION

How to Reach Lesvos

Depending on your location and preferences, there are several ways to get to Lesvos, one of Greece's biggest islands, via plane or water.

Through Air

By plane is the most practical method to go to Lesvos. The primary airport on the island, Mytilene International Airport (MJT), often referred to as Odysseas Elytis Airport, is situated around 8 kilometers south of the capital city of Mytilene. Both local and international flights are operated out of this airport.

1. From Athens: Athens International Airport (Eleftherios Venizelos) is the departure point for many daily flights. This is the quickest method to get from mainland Greece to the island since the flight takes around one hour.

2. Direct flights are also offered, departing Thessaloniki and arriving in Lesvos; the trip takes about one hour.

3. International Flights: Direct charter flights link Lesvos to major European destinations throughout the summer travel season. Seasonal flights are common in nations like the Netherlands, Germany, and the United Kingdom. It is normally better for visitors from outside of Europe to connect via Athens or Thessaloniki.

By Sea Ferries are another way to get to Lesvos, and they're a great choice for those who want to see the Aegean Sea. Though smaller ports like Sigri also provide connections, the major port is located in Mytilene.

1. From Piraeus Port in Athens: Ferries to Lesvos leave from Piraeus Port, which is close to Athens. Based on the kind of boat, the trip takes nine to twelve hours. Ferries often stay overnight, and on longer trips, cabins are frequently offered. Ferry travel is longer, but it provides beautiful scenery and the opportunity to feel the sea wind.

2. From Kavala: Lesvos may be reached by ferry from the port of Kavala in northern Greece; the trip takes around seven to ten hours.

3. Island Hopping: Lesvos is linked to the Dodecanese islands, such as Rhodes, and other islands in the northeastern Aegean, such as Chios, Lemnos, and Samos. A fantastic opportunity to see many Greek islands is by taking one of these interisland boats.

Ferry services may become congested, so it's advisable to reserve tickets in advance during the busiest travel months, which are July and August.

Transportation on the Island

Since Lesvos is a big island with a diverse terrain, having access to transportation is necessary for seeing the island's many regions.

Public Transportation

1. Buses: The major towns and tourist destinations in Lesvos are connected by an efficient bus system. Routes from Mytilene to important locations, including Molyvos, Petra, Kalloni, and Eressos, are served by the KTEL bus service. Summer bus timetables are more frequent, whereas winter bus schedules are less frequent. Although it's less expensive, it may not be able to reach farther-flung locations or provide the flexibility required for impromptu travel.

2. Taxis: You may either hail a taxi or schedule a pickup in advance in Mytilene and neighboring places. Although they can be an affordable option for long-distance travel, taxis may be a handy means to go to places that are harder to get to. In Greece, taxi costs are set by law, so it's advisable to find out the exact fee before you go, particularly for longer trips.

Rentals of cars and scooters
One of the finest ways to see Lesvos at your own leisure is to rent a vehicle or scooter.

1. Car Rentals: The city of Mytilene and the airport both have a number of rental companies. Numerous alternatives are available, from local operators to international brands like Hertz and Europcar. If you want to visit isolated villages or beaches, renting a vehicle is advised since public transportation could not get you to every location.

Although certain hilly places may have narrow or twisting roadways, the majority of the island's roads are in decent shape. Make sure to find out whether these regions are covered by the insurance on your rental automobile.

2. Scooter/Motorbike Rentals: For single visitors or couples wishing to explore the island's coastal roads, scooters and motorcycles are a common choice. They use less gasoline and are perfect for quick excursions or local visits. It's best suited for experienced riders, however, since certain routes may be challenging. Safety comes first.

3. Bicycle Rentals: Among cyclists, Lesvos is also gaining traction. It is possible to hire bicycles in Mytilene and nearby places. There are several official bike paths on the island, particularly those that round the Gulf of Kalloni; however, the mountainous terrain may make the ride difficult.

Island-wide Ferries

Local boats connect certain areas of Lesvos, providing an opportunity for tourists to explore more of the island's coastline. These quick boat trips provide beautiful views of the Aegean Sea in addition to transit between coastal villages.

Currency, Language, and Essential Travel Tips

Money

Lesvos is one of the Greek islands that utilizes the Euro (€). Particularly in smaller towns and villages, cash is extensively utilized. In bigger cities like Mytilene, the majority of establishments—including eateries, retail stores, and lodging—accept credit and debit cards; nonetheless, it's best to have cash while visiting rural regions.

1. ATMs: While they may be more difficult to locate in more isolated settlements, ATMs are easily accessible in Mytilene and bigger municipalities. It's important to be aware of transaction costs, particularly when using foreign credit cards, and to always have some cash on hand in case the machines malfunction.

2. Currency Exchange: Although exchange rates sometimes fluctuate, banks and a few travel firms in Mytilene provide foreign exchange services. In general, banks have better rates than nearby stores or lodging facilities.

Words

Greek is the official language of both Lesvos and the whole of Greece. Nonetheless, because of the island's tourism sector, English is often used at the main tourist locations, hotels, eateries, and retail establishments. In tourist locations, multilingual signage including both Greek and English is common.

1. Practical words: Although Greek is widely spoken, knowing a few fundamental words can improve your experience and demonstrate your respect for the people. Expressions like "Efharisto" (thank you), "Kalimera" (good morning), and "Parakalo" (please/you're welcome) are usually welcomed.

2. Communication applications: Translation applications may be quite helpful for tourists who might require help with the language, particularly in more rural locations where English competence may be restricted.

Crucial Advice for Travelers

1. Lesvos follows two different time zones: Eastern European Summer Time (EEST) during daylight saving time (UTC +3) and Eastern European Time (EET) throughout the winter

(UTC +2). If you are going from a different time zone, remember to set your clocks accordingly.

2. Electricity: Greece employs Type C and F plugs with a standard voltage of 230V. Make sure you pack the proper adaptor and voltage converter if you are coming from a nation that has a different plug type or voltage.

3. Health and Safety: Travelers may feel quite secure in Lesvos. Standard travel precautions do, however, still apply. In busy settings, make sure your valuables are safe, and don't leave personal belongings unattended at public spaces like beaches.

4. Medical Care: Mytilene General Hospital, the main healthcare facility on the island, is one of the medical facilities available. Particularly in bigger cities, pharmacies are widely dispersed, and the majority of pharmacists are fluent in English. Basic medical supplies are usually a good idea to have on hand, particularly if you're visiting far-flung locations.

5. Emergency Contact Information: Greece's basic emergency number is 112. You may call 100 to reach the local police. For emergency fire-related situations, call 199; for ambulance services, dial 166.

6. Tipping: Although not required in Greece, most service industries value tips. Tipping at restaurants is customary, with tips ranging from 5 to 10%. Rounding up the price in a cab is considered courteous.

7. Best Time to Visit: June to August, when the weather is hot and dry, is Lesvos' busiest travel month. Though the island is less congested and the weather is still excellent, May and September are good times to come if you want warmer temps and less tourists.

In summary

Lesvos is a convenient and easily accessible location for visitors arriving by air or sea. Once on the island, there are many ways to go about and see its breathtaking scenery, rich cultural history, and undiscovered treasures. Traveling about is easy and enables guests to take full use of the island, whether they want to utilize public transportation or hire a vehicle. With useful knowledge on money, language, and must-have travel advice, you'll be ready to make themost of your trip to Lesvos and guarantee a hassle-free and pleasurable stay.

CHAPTER THREE: TOP ATTRACTIONS IN LESVOS

The Iconic Mytilene Castle

On the island of Lesvos, the Mytilene Castle—among the biggest in the Mediterranean—is a noteworthy historical site. Perched on a hilltop, with sweeping views of both the city and the Aegean Sea, is the capital of Mytilene. Throughout history, its strategic location has made it an essential defensive system.

The Past and its Importance

The Byzantine era, about the sixth century AD, is when the fortress first appeared. Nevertheless, it has undergone several repairs and extensions by different governing forces, such as the Venetians, Genoese, and Ottomans. The greatest renovation took place in the 14th century under the reign of Lesvos' Genoese king, Francesco Gattilusio. Later, after capturing the island in 1462, the Ottomans strengthened the defenses.

Because of its advantageous position, Mytilene Castle has always been a military bastion that defended the island from invaders. During the Ottoman era, it served as both a jail and a home for the ruling class. Byzantine, Genoese, and Ottoman architectural characteristics may be seen in the castle's architecture, which represents the architectural influences of its many owners.

Architectural Elements

The castle is one of the biggest in the Mediterranean, spanning a vast area of over 200,000 square meters. The top, middle, and bottom castles make up its three portions. Each segment had a specific purpose; the lower castle had living and storage spaces, the middle section housed administrative structures, and the high half served military and defensive reasons.

Some of Mytilene Castle's main attractions are:

1. The Tower of the Queen: One of the best examples of Genoese military construction, this tower is lofty and formidable, providing superb views of the surroundings.

2. Subterranean Tunnels: The castle is notable for its subterranean tunnels, thought to have acted as escape routes and storerooms during times of siege.

3. Ottoman Structures: The castle still has a number of structures from the Ottoman period, such as a mosque and a bathhouse, which highlight the island's centuries-long cultural variety.

Experience of Visitors
Mytilene Castle is a popular tourist destination and remains available to tourists today. A modest

museum on the property is home to relics from many eras in the castle's history, such as antique weaponry, ceramics, and architectural pieces. The grounds of the castle are ideal for a stroll, enabling guests to explore its walls, turrets, and courtyards and take in the rich historical atmosphere.

During summer, the castle is a popular destination for both residents and visitors since it offers cultural activities including music concerts and theatrical productions. A must-see sight for visitors to Lesvos, Mytilene Castle combines historical importance with breathtaking scenery.

The Petrified Forest of Lesvos

One of the most remarkable natural wonders on the island is the Petrified Forest of Lesvos, which is recognized as a UNESCO Global Geopark. With fossilized trees that date back 20 million years, this forest in Lesvos' Sigri region provides a unique window into the island's geological past.

Geological Importance

About 20 million years ago, during the Late Oligocene to Early Miocene epoch, the Lesvos Petrified Forest came into being. Lesvos's rich subtropical woods were blanketed in ash deposits and large lava flows during this period due to volcanic activity in the Aegean area. The trees were protected by the volcanic ash, which sparked the petrification process, which turned the trees into stone by gradually replacing the organic content with minerals.

The forest's exceptional preservation makes it one of the biggest petrified forests in the world. Numerous petrified trees, some of which are more than 20 meters tall, are still standing in their original locations. Because silica makes up the majority of the petrified trunks, they resemble stones, and minute characteristics of the trees, including growth rings and bark, are often still discernible.

Experience of Visitors

There are several publicly accessible, recognized areas throughout the vast expanse of the Petrified Forest. The Natural History Museum of the Lesvos Petrified Forest is situated in the town of Sigri, which is close to the most accessible locations. This museum provides a thorough examination of the history of volcanic activity in the area, the development of the petrified forest, and the paleontological value of the fossils.

Take guided trips through the fossilized forest and see several areas, such as Plaka Park, which has the highest concentration of petrified trees. Many of the trees in this area are still standing straight and reach heights of over 20 meters and 3 meters in diameter. Other notable areas include Nissiopi Islet, accessible by boat, where visitors can observe petrified tree trunks and roots along the island's coastline.

Walking pathways are accessible for anyone who prefers to explore the forest independently, with signs offering extensive information about the fossils and the geological processes that generated them. The paths give amazing views of the surrounding volcanic environment and the neighboring Aegean Sea, allowing for a picturesque and instructive experience.

The Museum of Natural History

Anyone interested in the geological history of the island should definitely visit the Natural History Museum. It has interactive displays that describe the island's rich biodiversity while the forest was alive, in addition to exhibits on the volcanic activity that caused the forest to become petrified. The exhibit of fossilized leaves, plants, and tree trunks allows guests to get a close-up view of this prehistoric subtropical habitat.

The museum offers educational programs, workshops, and research initiatives, all of which contribute significantly to the preservation and promotion of the forest as a worldwide geological heritage site.

The Monastery of Saint Raphael

Northeast of Mytilene, on a hill close to the settlement of Thermi, is the holy Monastery of Saint Raphael. It is one of the most prominent spiritual monuments in Lesvos and is a key pilgrimage site for Orthodox Christians.

The Significance of Religion in History

Three saints, Saint Raphael, Saint Nicholas, and Saint Irene, are honored in the monastery. It is thought that they were martyred there in the fifteenth century during the Ottoman era.

Tradition has it that Saint Irene was a young girl who died as a martyr beside Saint Raphael, the monastery's abbot, and Saint Nicholas, a deacon.

Early in the 1960s, local villagers began to find their relics after experiencing visions and dreams in which the saints revealed their final resting places. The monastery gained religious significance once the relics were found, and pilgrims now go there in search of miracles and spiritual healing.

Architectural Elements

The Saint Raphael main church, smaller chapels, and monastic cells are among the structures that make up the monastery complex. The architecture has classic Byzantine influences and is elegant yet simple. The inside of the cathedral is embellished with exquisite paintings and icons showing the lives of the saints and episodes from Orthodox Christian traditions.

The crypt, where the relics of the three saints are preserved, is a major aspect of the pilgrimage experience. In order to get blessings from the saints, visitors frequently light candles or leave offerings in the crypt.

Journey and Guest Experience

The Monastery of Saint Raphael is an important pilgrimage destination, particularly during the Easter season and on April 9th, which is the feast day of Saint Raphael. Thousands of pilgrims from Greece and other countries visit the monastery during these periods to pay respects to the remains and take part in religious rituals.

In addition to its religious significance, the monastery welcomes guests into a tranquil setting. The site offers expansive views of the Aegean Sea, hills, and olive fields in the area. The well-maintained gardens and courtyards enhance the monastery's quiet environment, making it a great spot for thought and meditation.

The monastery is open to visitors of all religions, and guided excursions that delve into the site's history and the lives of the saints are offered. The monastery's tiny museum provides a deeper understanding of the island's religious heritage by showcasing religious artifacts, icons, and vestments.

In summary, Lesvos is rich in cultural, historical, and natural attractions, with the Mytilene Castle, Petrified Forest, and Monastery of Saint Raphael being among its most iconic landmarks. These sites offer a glimpse into the island's diverse past, geological wonders, and spiritual importance, making them must-see destinations for any traveler exploring the island.

CHAPTER FOUR: BEST BEACHES IN LESVOS

Vatera Beach

Vatera Beach, situated on the southern coast of Lesvos, is one of the longest and most popular beaches on the island, running for nearly 8 kilometers. It is well-known for its crystal-clear waters, fine sand, and organized amenities, making it a favorite among both locals and tourists seeking a relaxing seaside experience.

Characteristics and atmosphere

Vatera Beach features a blend of fine sand and small pebbles, and it slopes gently into the Aegean Sea's crystal-clear blue waters. Even in the busiest summer months, the beach's length provides plenty of space, making it the perfect choice for people who want to avoid crowded areas. Vatera has received multiple Blue Flag awards for its exceptional cleanliness of the water, which is a testament to its high environmental and safety standards.

With shallow waters close to the shore that are ideal for kids and non-swimmers, the beach is family-friendly. The sea gradually gets deeper as you go deeper, which makes it perfect for activities like swimming and snorkeling. The backdrop of verdant hills and olive groves accentuates Vatera Beach's natural beauty, resulting in a tranquil and picturesque setting.

Facilities and Amenities

Vatera Beach has all the amenities needed to guarantee a relaxing day by the water. Along the shoreline are several beach bars, tavernas, and cafés that serve a variety of food and beverages, including regional Greek cuisine. Visitors may unwind in luxury by renting sunbeds and umbrellas from a number of the seaside businesses.

Vatera Beach has a number of rental stations that provide gear for water sports enthusiasts to engage in activities including windsurfing, kayaking, and paddleboarding. It's a fantastic place for novices to try their hand at these sports because of the calm and shallow seas.

In addition, there are several lodging alternatives close to the beach that suit a range of budgets, from private villas to hotels and guesthouses. Vatera is not overly developed, maintaining a laid-back atmosphere despite its popularity, which adds to its appeal for those seeking a more tranquil beach experience.

Surrounding Attractions

In addition to its natural beauty, Vatera Beach is close to several interesting cultural and historical sites. Just a short drive away is the Ancient Temple of Dionysus, an archaeological site dating back to the 5th century BC, offering a glimpse into the island's rich history. Visitors can also explore the nearby Polichnitos Hot Springs, one of the hottest natural springs in Europe, known for their therapeutic properties.

The beach's location makes it a great base for exploring the southern part of Lesvos, with several charming villages nearby, such as Vrisa, which features traditional stone houses and small tavernas where visitors can enjoy authentic local cuisine.

Skala Eressos Beach

Located on the western coast of Lesvos, Skala Eressos Beach is a stunning 3-kilometer-long stretch of sand, widely regarded as one of the most beautiful and unspoiled beaches on the island. This beach holds special cultural significance as the birthplace of the ancient Greek poet Sappho, and it attracts a diverse range of visitors, from families to independent travelers, especially those interested in alternative lifestyles and culture.

Characteristics and atmosphere

Skala Eressos Beach is notable for its large stretch of excellent, black sand and deep, clear seas. The beach is placed against a background of steep cliffs, with the settlement of Skala Eressos only a few meters away, offering a scenic setting. Unlike more marketed beaches, Skala Eressos has preserved much of its natural appeal, and its somewhat secluded position keeps it calmer than many other beaches on the island.

The beach offers a warm and open attitude, and it has long been a favorite destination for LGBTQ+ vacationers. It's also well-known for its yoga retreats, meditation institutes, and holistic health programs, making it a magnet for individuals interested in wellness and alternative lifestyles. The laid-back attitude of Skala Eressos draws guests who desire a more calm and informal beach experience.

Facilities and Amenities

Despite its natural character, Skala Eressos Beach provides a decent choice of services to guarantee a pleasant visit. There are various tavernas, cafés, and taverns along the seafront, many of which are constructed on stilts above the sand, affording spectacular views of the sea. These restaurants feature a wide range of cuisines to suit different palates, from foreign to traditional Greek.

Water activities like windsurfing and paddleboarding are accessible for those who wish to explore the sea; rental facilities are situated directly on the beach. Though there is plenty of room for guests to spread out their towels on the beach if they would rather have a more natural experience, sunbeds and umbrellas may be hired.

There are many places to stay in the surrounding hamlet of Skala Eressos, ranging from boutique hotels to guesthouses that are more affordable. Along with stores and small markets, the hamlet boasts a lively nightlife scene, especially in the summer when the beach draws a greater number of foreign visitors.

Historical and Cultural Significance

Because Skala Eressos is linked to Sappho, one of the finest lyric poets of classical Greece, it has a particular position in Greek culture. The region is rich in history, and tourists may explore the ancient Eressos ruins, which still include the remains of temples and other buildings.

Particularly in the summer, the beach often holds literary events, music festivals, and art exhibits for individuals with an interest in art and culture. Skala Eressos is a unique location on the island, combining natural beauty with a rich cultural heritage thanks to its laid-back bohemian character.

Petra Beach

Located on Lesvos' northern shore, Petra Beach is one of the island's most easily accessible and kid-friendly beaches. The hamlet of Petra, which is home to the beach, is well-known for its picturesque alleyways, classic tavernas, and the remarkable rock formation topped by the Church of Panagia Glykofilousa.

Specifications and Ambience

Perfect for families and kids, Petra Beach has lovely sandy waves and shallow, warm seas. With its gentle sand and serene seas, the roughly 2-kilometer beach is the perfect place for swimming and tanning. For many meters, the water is still quite shallow, making it a secure place for children to play and swim.

The hamlet has a vibrant vibe due to its close proximity to the beach, particularly during the summer when both residents and visitors swarm to take advantage of the pleasant weather and seaside eateries. Petra Beach is large enough to provide a tranquil experience while being a well-liked site, with plenty of space for guests to select their own area along the coast.

Facilities and Amenities

Petra Beach is well managed, offering a variety of eateries, cafés, and bars along the shoreline in addition to loungers and umbrellas for hire. Eating out without having to leave the beach is made simple by the abundance of fresh seafood and traditional Greek cuisine available at the local eateries. Additionally, there are several beach bars that provide light fare and cool beverages all day long.

Rentable water toys include jet skis, paddleboards, and pedal boats for individuals who want to go active on the water. Beginners may attempt water sports in the calm seas, and because of the diversity of marine life in the vicinity, snorkeling is popular in certain parts of the beach.

Petra Town has a wide variety of lodging alternatives, from high-end hotels to more reasonably priced flats and guesthouses. It's simple for guests to enjoy the beach and sea during their stay since so many of the hotels are close to the beach by foot.

Historical and Cultural Significance

The massive rock structure that dominates the scenery is one of Petra Beach's most outstanding characteristics. The Church of Panagia Glykofilousa is perched atop this rock and can be ascended via 114 stone steps. The church is a well-liked location for both locals and tourists because it provides expansive views of the village and the surrounding coastline. A common sight in pictures of the island is the church and the rock, which serve as iconic representations of Petra.

The village of Petra itself is rich in history, offering a window into the island's past through its winding streets and traditional architecture. When summertime rolls around, visitors may stroll around the village square and take in traditional music performances in addition to shopping for handcrafted items, jewelry, and artwork.

In summary

Greece's most stunning beaches can be found in Lesvos, and each one has something special to offer tourists. Skala Eressos Beach provides a more bohemian and culturally diverse experience, while Vatera Beach is ideal for those looking for a long, sandy length with contemporary facilities and clean waves.

CHAPTER FIVE: EXPLORING LESVOS'S NATURAL WONDERS

Hot Springs of Eftalou

One of Lesvos' most well-known natural landmarks, the Hot Springs of Eftalou, are close to the northern town of Molyvos and lure tourists looking for restorative and therapeutic services. The hot spring water's abundance in minerals, such as sulfur, which has long been linked to health advantages, makes the springs renowned for their curative qualities. For those who want to take advantage of Lesvos's natural healing resources in addition to its scenic splendor, these natural thermal baths provide a unique experience.

Features of the Springs

With temperatures as high as 46°C (114°F), the Eftalou hot springs are particularly soothing in the winter months or on calm nights. The hot pool is located in the main bathing area, which is housed in a modest, traditional stone structure. The warm water's rising steam adds to the tranquility and calm of the basic but evocative décor of the bath.

A few meters away, the hot waters run into the sea for those who would rather enjoy it outside. Bathers are able to take advantage of the natural blend of warm and cold water created by this, as well as the refreshing Aegean air. This revitalizing contrast of sea and hot water is often suggested to improve circulation and relaxation.

Therapeutic Advantages

Because of the high concentration of sulfur and other minerals in the water, it is thought that the Eftalou hot springs provide a number of health advantages. These minerals are well-known for their ability to relieve joint pain, arthritis, and muscular stiffness, as well as skin disorders including psoriasis and eczema. After a strenuous day of trekking or island exploration, many people come to the springs to relieve diseases, while others just enjoy the very soothing experience.

Although there hasn't been much research done on the springs' therapeutic qualities recently, local custom indicates that the waters' healing powers have been used for ages. A wonderful way to relax and take in some of Lesvos' natural beauty is to bathe in the hot waters, whether or not people are there for medical purposes.

Getting There and Insider Advice

The Eftalou hot springs are a popular day trip destination for people staying in the vicinity since they are readily accessible from the adjacent town of Molyvos by vehicle or public transportation. The springs are available all year round, but people are most drawn to experience them in the fall and winter when the chilly water and crisp air provide for a striking contrast.

It is recommended that guests pack swimsuits and towels, as they are not usually available on the premises. It's also a good idea to bring bottled water and other needs since the bathhouse is pretty basic. Although there is seldom a throng at the springs, it is advisable to arrive early in the morning or late at night to avoid the busiest times.

Olive Groves and Scenic Trails
Large tracts of the island of Lesvos are covered with olive orchards, which are renowned for being essential to the island's economy and natural beauty. The island is one of Greece's main producers of olive oil since it has more than 11 million olive trees on it. In addition to providing tourists with a sense of the island's agricultural past, the olive trees allow them to explore some of Lesvos' most picturesque hiking paths.

Lesvos's Olive Groves

The olive trees of Lesvos are largely of the Kolovi kind, which is unique to the island. Many of these trees are hundreds of years old, and they provide excellent olives and olive oil that are prized for their taste and nutritional content. A distinctive aspect of the terrain of Lesvos, especially in the central and southern regions, are the olive orchards.

Hikers may stroll along the rustic trails that meander between the woods to discover these groves on foot. An aura of tranquility and reminiscence is created by the aroma of the olive trees and the sight of the silver-green leaves gleaming in the sunshine. The sensory experience is enhanced by the wildflowers and herbs that are scattered throughout several of the woods.

Trails for Hiking among Olive Groves

There is a vast network of hiking routes across Lesvos, many of which go through or next to the island's olive trees. The Petra to Molyvos path is one of the most well-liked hiking trails since it provides breathtaking views of the surrounding Aegean Sea and the hills covered with olive trees. This route is an excellent opportunity to get some fitness in addition to taking in Lesvos' natural beauty since it is well-marked and appropriate for hikers of all ability levels.

Other noteworthy pathways include the Achladeri Forest track and the Vatousa to Agra route, which both allow hikers to experience walking through olive trees and other natural settings. These paths are open all year round, but they are especially lovely in the spring when the wildflowers blossom.

Some nearby farms provide tours and tastings where guests may see the olive oil-making process up close and taste freshly created oil, perfect for people who are curious in the island's olive oil production. This offers a better comprehension of the island's farming customs and a special bond with the land.

The Significance of Olive Oil in Culture

For thousands of years, olive oil has been a vital component of the island's economy and culture. Olive oil is a way of life in Lesvos, not simply a commodity. The production of olive oil is the main industry in many of the island's towns, and during harvest season, it's not unusual to observe residents taking care of their olive trees or laboring in the presses.

Every year, in late fall and early winter, there is a bustling and joyous olive harvest. During this time, guests visiting Lesvos may see the customary methods of harvesting olives, which include catching the olives with nets as they are gently knocked from the branches.

Birdwatching at Kalloni Salt Pans

Situated in the center of Lesvos, the Kalloni Salt Pans are an essential natural environment on the island, especially for avian aficionados. Nestled between swamps and marshes, these enormous salt pans serve as an essential resting place for migratory birds making their way from Europe to Africa. They are a part of the Gulf of Kalloni, a protected area designated by Natura 2000 because to its high biodiversity.

Highlights of Birdwatching

Being home to an incredible diversity of bird species, the salt pans and associated wetlands are among the most significant birding locations in the Mediterranean. The salt pans are brimming with flamingos, pelicans, herons, and a variety of waders throughout the main migratory seasons, which are spring and fall.

The big flock of Greater Flamingos that gathers near the salt pans is one of the most famous sights. Birdwatchers go from all over the globe to see the breathtaking visual spectacle created by the pink color of the flamingos against the blue sky and white salt flats.

The salt pans are home to uncommon species such the Glossy Ibis, Black Stork, Little Egret, and Stone Curlew in addition to flamingos. Raptors that hunt in the region, such Marsh Harriers and Short-toed Eagles, are also visible to birdwatchers.

Availability and Ideal Times to Go

Bicycles and cars may easily reach the Kalloni Salt Pans, where a number of overlooks provide unhindered views of the birds and their habitats. Around the salt pans, there are also setups for birding hides, which provide cover for watchers and guarantee that the birds are not startled.

Since the largest range of species may be observed during the migratory periods of March to May and September to October, these are the ideal times to visit the salt pans. But since resident species like Greater Flamingos are constantly there and may frequently be spotted all year round, birdwatchers can visit the salt pans any time of year.

Preservation and the Significance of the Environment

The salt pans are essential to the local ecology because they provide habitat for a wide range of animals, including fish and invertebrates, in addition to birds. The Ramsar Convention protects the region, and conservation initiatives are implemented to guarantee that the habitat will continue to support the variety of species that depend on it.

During the summer, tourists may often see the traditional process of harvesting salt, which still involves using salt pans. This age-old custom is being followed today in accordance with the requirements of the species, preserving the fragile ecosystem's balance.

In summary

Lesvos is home to several natural treasures, like as the healing Eftalou Hot Springs, the peaceful olive orchards, and the world-famous birding at the Kalloni Salt Pans. Lesvos is a popular destination for outdoor enthusiasts and nature lovers due to its many natural features, which provide tourists exceptional chances to engage with the island's rich terrain.

CHAPTER SIX: LESVOS'S HIDDEN GEMS

The Charming Village of Agiasos

Nestled on the foothills of Mount Olympus in Lesvos, the charming town of Agiasos is a hidden treasure renowned for its traditional architecture, rich cultural legacy, and long history. One of the most charming locations on the island, this town is tucked away among lush hills and attracts travelers looking to see a more genuine, off-the-beaten-path side of Lesvos.

Conventional styles and ambience

Agiasos is well known for its colorful homes, winding cobblestone alleyways, and exceptionally well-preserved Ottoman-style buildings. The town is a labyrinth of narrow lanes dotted with ancient houses, the majority of which have colorful painted shutters and elaborately carved wooden balconies.

The village's design promotes exploration, with charming courtyards, blooming flowerpots, and surprising vistas of the hills beyond around every corner.

Agiasos's center square, or plateia, is home to the magnificent Church of Panagia, one of the most significant pilgrimage destinations in the region. The church honors Mary and is home to a famous religious artwork of the Madonna from the Byzantine period that is said to have healing powers. Because of this, Agiasos is a popular destination for Orthodox Christians, especially on August 15th when the hamlet celebrates a large religious celebration in honor of the Assumption of the Virgin Mary.

Folk traditions and handicrafts
Agiasos is known for its long legacy of handicrafts, particularly woodcarving and ceramics. Since the town has long been a hub for craftsmanship, guests

are welcome to tour any one of the many workshops where skilled workers continue to carry out their age-old skills. The pottery of Agiasos is especially known for its vibrant colors and elaborate patterns, while the woodcarvers make wonderfully carved furniture, holy icons, and ornamental objects.

The folk theater and music traditions of Agiasos are also well-known. The hamlet has a rich tradition of hosting festivals and theatrical productions to honor the local way of life. Those who are fortunate enough to visit Agiasos during a festival may take in live bouzouki music, see traditional folk dances, and experience the warmth of the residents.

Nature and Pathways for Hiking

Because Agiasos is bordered by dense woods, especially those of pine and chestnut trees, it is a great place for hikers to start their journey. From the hamlet, one of the most well-liked treks ascends

Mount Olympus, where breathtaking sweeping views of the island and the Aegean Sea await. Hikers may have a serene and beautiful experience as they go through lush woodlands that are scattered with little chapels and springs.

Ancient Theatre of Mytilene

One of the most significant archeological monuments on Lesvos is the Ancient Theatre of Mytilene, which provides tourists with a window into the rich classical past of the island. The theater, which is said to have been one of the biggest and most spectacular in the ancient Greek world, is situated on the hill of Agia Kyriaki in Mytilene and dates back to the third century BC.

Historical Importance

When Mytilene was a flourishing political and cultural hub in the Aegean, the theater was first constructed during the Hellenistic era. It is thought to have been around the same size as the famous

Theater of Epidaurus, with seating for about 15,000 people. During the Roman era, the building hosted public gatherings, theatrical productions, and maybe even gladiatorial fights.

The acoustics of the theater are said to have so impressed the Roman Emperor Pompey that he used its layout for the theaters he constructed in Rome. With a spacious cavea (seating area) constructed into the hill's natural slope, the theater's architecture was exceptional for its period and offered views over the port and the city of Mytilene as well as good acoustics.

Present State and Repair

The orchestra (stage area) and some of the seats have been excavated and are visible to tourists, despite the fact that the majority of the theater is now in ruins. Archaeologists are still striving to find and save more of the theater's original elements as part of restoration works.

The site is an amazing example of the magnificence of ancient Greek architecture, even in its unfinished form. Explore the remains and try to picture what it might have been like to see a show here more than two millennia ago.

The theater's usage for cultural events, such as plays and concerts, has increased recently, reinstating its status as an artistic facility. The intimate and magnificent ambiance created by the surroundings and acoustics of the old theater makes attending an event there a very unique experience.

Taking a Look at the Ancient Theatre

It's easy to get to the Ancient Theatre of Mytilene from the city center, and it's a good idea to combine a visit to the theater with a stroll around the ancient town. Though historical background is provided via information boards, it's worthwhile to hire a guide or take a tour to fully appreciate the importance of the location.

The Museum of Industrial Olive Oil Production

An interesting place to visit that provides information on the island's lengthy history of olive farming and olive oil manufacturing is the Museum of Industrial Olive Oil Manufacturing in the town of Agia Paraskevi. Not only is olive oil fundamental to Greek cooking, but it also plays a significant role in the island's economy and sense of culture.

Background Information in History

The museum, located in a renovated olive oil mill, offers a thorough look at how this industry changed throughout time. Lesvos has been a hub of olive oil production for generations. The Piraeus Bank Group Cultural Foundation founded the museum with the goal of conserving and showcasing Lesvos' industrial past, with a particular emphasis on the automation of olive oil production during the early 20th century.

The 1910-built mill used steam-powered equipment, which was a major departure from the customary techniques of pressing olives. The museum's displays emphasize how industrial processes replaced human labor, enabling higher production quantities and efficiency.

Displays and Equipment

The museum offers visitors the opportunity to examine the original presses, grinding stones, and boilers used in the olive oil manufacturing process. Several of this meticulously refurbished equipment is on exhibit with pictures and records that detail the workings of the manufacturing process.

Multimedia displays in the museum explore the history of olive oil production on the island, spanning from prehistoric times to the present day.

Visitors may learn about the many phases of olive oil manufacturing, from harvesting the olives to extracting and bottling the oil, via interactive exhibits.

The museum has a section devoted to the social and economic issues of producing olive oil in addition to the technology. This section of the exhibition delves on the everyday uses of olive oil by the Lesvos people, including its usage in cooking, medicinal, and religious rites.

Olive oil's cultural and economic significance
On Lesvos, olive oil has long represented the island's ties to the land and its customs and has been more than simply a commodity. The museum highlights the importance of olive oil to local rituals and festivals, as well as its place in Mediterranean cuisine.

The museum's emphasis on Agia Paraskevi's cooperative movement, which was essential in the growth of the olive oil sector, is among its most intriguing features. Local farmers were able to invest in new equipment and pool their resources thanks to the cooperative, which significantly improved their production capacity and made them more competitive on the international market.

Going to the Museum

Situated in a wonderfully renovated structure that has maintained much of its original character is the Museum of Industrial Olive Oil Production. The mill is open for self-guided tours, with information available in both Greek and English. The museum is a fantastic place for people of all ages to visit since it also organizes temporary exhibits and educational events.

Exploring the nearby hamlet of Agia Paraskevi is equally worthwhile since it provides a tranquil look into rural Lesvos life. In addition to dining at a neighborhood taverna and sampling the island's renowned olive oil, visitors may take in the picturesque views of the olive fields that dot the surrounding terrain.

In summary

Lesvos is brimming with undiscovered attractions that provide a more thorough grasp of the island's natural beauty, history, and culture. These attractions offer visitors distinctive and enriching experiences that go beyond the typical tourist spots. From the quaint village of Agiasos, with its rich handicraft traditions and picturesque hiking trails, to the historic grandeur of the Theatre of Mytilene and the thought-provoking exhibits at the Museum of Industrial Olive Oil Production.

CHAPTER SEVEN: THE FLAVORS OF LESVOS: A CULINARY JOURNEY

Traditional Dishes and Local Delicacies

Recognized for its lush terrain and rich gastronomic legacy, Lesvos has a wide selection of customary meals that accentuate the distinct tastes of the island. Numerous recipes are based on Greek and Ottoman cuisine, with a focus on using foods that are fresh and easily obtained in the area.

Kiskek

Kiskek, sometimes known as keshkek, is a traditional slow-cooked stew made with wheat and meat, often served on special occasions. It is one of the most recognizable meals in Lesvos. It's made of cracked wheat and meat (typically chicken or lamb) that's simmered in a big pot for hours until it's tender and creamy. Served on religious feasts or festivals like Panagia's Day (August 15th), the meal is a sign of festivity. The flavors combine throughout the lengthy cooking process, which includes frequent stirring, to provide a filling and cozy supper.

Pastes Sardeles (salted sea bass)

Sardeles pastes, or salted sardines, are another must-try treat. Some of the best sardines in the Mediterranean may be found in the seas of Lesvos, especially in the Gulf of Kalloni. These little, tasty fish are typically served with ouzo after being freshly caught and salted. Traditionally, the sardines are served as a meze, or appetizer, with bread or salad on the side and a dressing of olive oil. Both residents and tourists love this meal because of its simplicity, which highlights the freshness of the fish.

Zucchini Pie, or Kolokythopita

A savory zucchini pie known as kolokythopita is another well-liked dish that showcases the island's longstanding heritage of vegetarian cooking. The pie is composed of thin phyllo dough layers that are filled with feta cheese, shredded zucchini, eggs, and herbs like dill and mint. Kolokythopita, when baked to golden perfection, is a tasty and light meal that works well for a meze spread or lunch.

Loukoumades

Lesvos residents love loukoumades, which are deep-fried dough balls covered with honey, cinnamon, and chopped almonds. These sugary confections have a light texture, crisp outside, and tender inside. A popular dish during festivals, loukoumades are often offered as a component of festivities. They are seductive with their rich taste and golden look, particularly when coupled with a strong cup of Greek coffee.

Olive Oil and Ouzo: Lesvos's Signature Products

The cuisine of Lesvos is closely linked to its two most well-known exports, ouzo and olive oil.

Olive Oil

Lesvos's perfect climate and rich soil are responsible for producing some of Greece's greatest olive oil. Ancient olive groves dot the island's terrain, with many of them harboring trees that date back hundreds of years. Native to Lesvos, the Kolovi olive type yields an exceptional oil valued for its somewhat peppery and fruity taste.

A staple of Lesvos cuisine, olive oil can be found in almost every dish, from simple salads to intricate stews. Locals often eat a slice of freshly baked bread as a light snack or starter, drizzled in olive oil and sprinkled with sea salt and oregano. Rich in heart-healthy lipids and antioxidants, Lesvos olive oil is well-known for its health advantages and is a mainstay of the Mediterranean diet.

Tasting sessions and tours of the island's olive oil mills are two ways that visitors to Lesvos may learn about the island's olive oil culture. Visitors may taste a variety of olive oils and learn about the traditional production processes from several of the island's tiny, family-run producers.

Lesvos is also the origin of ouzo, the national anise-flavored liquor of Greece. The island is home to some of the nation's most well-known ouzo distilleries, and the people there are very proud of the quality of their output. To give it a characteristic liquorice taste, anise seeds and other fragrant herbs are distilled with alcohol to create ouzo.

The town of Plomari on the island of Lesvos is the source of one of the most well-known Ouzo brands, Ouzo Plomari. Many people refer to the hamlet as the center of Ouzo manufacturing, and tourists may take a tour of the Ouzo Barbayanni Distillery to discover more about the background and method of creating this renowned alcoholic beverage.

Traditionally savored as an aperitif, ouzo is often served with a dash of water, which distorts the otherwise clear drink. Small meze appetizers like grilled octopus, cheese, and olives are usually served with it. Many people believe that a trip to Lesvos is not complete unless they relax at a taverna by the shore and have an ouzo while watching the sun set over the Aegean shore.

Best Restaurants and Taverns in Lesvos

The eating scene on Lesvos is full of quaint pubs, intimate diners, and fine dining establishments that highlight the island's extensive culinary legacy. Here are some of the greatest places to eat on the island, ranging from little coastal nooks to undiscovered hamlet treasures.

Vafios Taverna (Molyvos)

Taverna Vafios, a well-known restaurant with breathtaking views of the surrounding hills and traditional food, is situated in the town of Molyvos. The taverna prepares traditional meals such as lamb cooked in clay pots, fresh fish, and different meze platters using products that are found locally. The goat stew, a soft dish that is slow-cooked and perfectly captures the robust tastes of rural Lesvos, is one of the menu's highlights. At Taverna Vafios, the terrace provides the ideal atmosphere for a leisurely dinner while taking in the stunning surroundings.

Nikou Ouzeri tou (Mytilene)

In Mytilene, the Lesvos capital, visit Ouzeri tou Nikou for a genuine meze and ouzo experience. A modest and modest ouzeri (a tavern that specializes in ouzo and small meals) offering a selection of classic meze, such as grilled octopus, fried sardines, and tzatziki. The fact that locals visit this location often is evidence of its excellence and genuineness. It's a terrific spot to enjoy the community spirit of Greek dining, where sharing dishes and chatting is the norm, thanks to the vibrant setting and pleasant service.

Gatos (Kallonis Scala)

Located in the Skala Kallonis town, Gatos is a seafood enthusiast's dream come true. This taverna serves fresh seafood that is harvested daily in the Gulf of Kalloni and is well-known for its sardines, which are a specialty of the area. Gatos offers a variety of seafood meals, such as baked mussels and grilled calamari, in addition to sardines. The quality of the seafood is highlighted by the straightforward methods, and the waterfront setting adds to the dining experience's allure.

The Petra Women's Cooperative (Petra)

Visit the Women's Cooperative of Petra in the Petra Hamlet for a unique eating experience. Local women who wished to save and share traditional recipes—many of which had been handed down through the generations—founded this cooperative. The menu offers a variety of regional sweets, including ravani (a syrup-soaked semolina cake) and home-cooked meals like moussaka and stuffed veggies. It seems like you're eating in someone's house since everything is created from scratch using local, fresh ingredients. The decor is cozy and inviting.

Mougou Kafeneio (Plomari)

A must-visit for anybody in Plomari, the Ouzo capital, is Kafeneio tou Mougou. This classic coffee shop, or kafeneio, is well-known for its meze and ouzo combinations. Simple yet excellent, the menu features small servings of eggplant salad, cheese saganaki, and marinated anchovies. With its rustic charm and wooden tables, the environment is warm and inviting, making it the ideal place for a light lunch or an afternoon snack.

In summary

Lesvos is a place where the history, culture, and natural abundance of the island are profoundly ingrained in the culinary traditions. Lesvos's tastes provide a distinctive culinary experience, ranging from robust traditional meals like kiskek and salted sardines to the island's hallmark goods, olive oil and ouzo. Discovering the handcrafted goods of a nearby cooperative or enjoying a meal at a taverna by the sea in Skala Kallonis, travelers are certain to be mesmerized by the genuineness and excellence of the island's food.

CHAPTER EIGHT: OUTDOOR ACTIVITIES AND ADVENTURES

The charming island of Lesvos in the northeastern Aegean Sea has a wide range of outdoor activities to suit the interests of thrill-seekers, nature enthusiasts, and anybody wishing to take in the breath-taking scenery of the island. Lesvos offers an abundance of hiking, cycling, sailing, and ecotourism options due to its varied topography, pristine waterways, and abundant wildlife.

Hiking and Cycling in Lesvos

Lesvos is home to a vast network of hiking routes that meander across its breathtaking scenery, which includes tranquil seaside pathways and steep highlands. The island's rich history, which includes historic settlements and old ruins along many of the routes, complements its stunning natural surroundings.

Well-liked Paths for Hiking

1. The Path of Olympus

Hiking trails like this one that ascend Mount Olympus are among the most well-liked on the island. The climb gives breathtaking sweeping views of the surrounding countryside and the Aegean Sea. Hikers who successfully complete the often difficult climb are rewarded with breath-taking views and the opportunity to discover rare plants and animals. The track is well-marked and appropriate for both novice and expert hikers seeking a fairly challenging journey.

2. Coastal Path from Molyvos to Eftalou

Visitors love this trek along the shore, which begins in the quaint town of Molyvos. The track hugs the coast, offering breathtaking views of the ocean and the lush surroundings. Hikers may explore isolated beaches and rocky coves along the way, which makes it a great path for anybody who wants to take in the beautiful landscape and the chance to bathe in the cool waters. The trek is ideal for a half-day excursion since it is just around 6 kilometers long and can be finished in two hours.

3. Tsiknias Mountain to Agiasos

The second-highest mountain on the island, Mount Tsiknias, is reached by route from Agiasos settlement. In addition to providing a window into traditional village life, the climb gives views of the native vegetation and fauna. The course has a moderate difficulty rating and is around 10 kilometers long. Hikers may take in the distinctive rock formations and rich greenery as they rise, leading to a viewpoint with breath-taking views.

Adventures on Two Wheels

Another wonderful method to discover Lesvos's natural beauty is via bicycle. There are several different bike routes on the island, ranging from easy beach circuits to strenuous mountain treks. Mountain and electric bikes are available for hire from a number of local rental businesses, making it simple for guests to hit the trails.

1. Cycling Routes Along the Coastal Line

The coastal paths around Kalloni Bay provide beautiful scenery and mild topography for a more leisurely ride. Cycling along the coast's bike route lets riders take in the stunning beaches and historic fishing communities. This is a leisurely-paced route that is appropriate for all ability levels.

2. North American Mountain Biking

Excellent mountain bike tracks may be found in the northern region of Lesvos, especially near Molyvos, for those who are looking for adventure. There are rough trails, hard climbs, and enjoyable descents in this diverse terrain. Cycling enthusiasts may discover undiscovered routes that lead to magnificent vantage spots with views of the surrounding countryside and the sea.

3. Tours for Cyclists with Guides

Guided bicycle trips that give insights into the island's natural beauty, history, and culture are available from a number of local tour companies. In addition to offering travelers an enjoyable ride, these trips often include stops at historic towns, olive orchards, and vineyards in the area.

Sailing and Water Sports

Lesvos is a great place for sailing and other water activities because of its crystal-clear seas. Many beaches and secluded bays can be found throughout the island's coastline, making boat exploration an ideal activity.

Cruising

1. Services for Charters

There are many charter companies that provide half-day and full-day sailing excursions around Lesvos. Sailboat rentals and guided sailing trips are available to visitors; the latter often make stops at secluded coves and beaches. Enjoying the breathtaking views of the coastline and the peace of the open ocean while sailing in the Aegean Sea is a great opportunity.

2. Boat rides at dusk

Sail into the sunset on a sunset cruise is one of the best parts of Lesvos. Usually leaving in the late afternoon, these excursions provide visitors the chance to take in the breathtaking view of the sun setting over the Aegean Sea. Dinner is often served on board on cruises, and it's always a spectacular affair with fresh seafood from the area and classic Greek fare.

3. Instruction in Sailing

A number of businesses provide sailing instruction to anyone who is interested in learning to sail. Whether you're a total beginner or want to improve, the majority of sessions teach fundamental navigation, sailing methods, and safety precautions.

Aquatic Sports

1. Kiteboarding and wind

Because of the ideal winds, the beaches of Lesvos, especially Petry and Skala Eressos, are well-liked places for windsurfing and kitesurfing. Both novice and expert surfers may rent equipment and take training from nearby schools. An adrenaline-seeking person's favorite sport is gliding over the waves in these breathtaking surroundings because of the excitement of it.

2. Snorkeling and Diving

Because of the abundance of marine life in the seas around Lesvos, diving and snorkeling are popular pastimes. Divers of all experience levels may hire equipment and take advantage of guided trips offered by the island's diving shops. Divers may explore rich underwater ecosystems on several reefs, as well as the submerged city of Daskalopetra, which are notable dive locations. Many beaches have shallow waters that are ideal for snorkeling, which allows people to see colorful fish and other marine life.

3. Canoeing

Another fantastic method to see Lesvos's coastline is via sea kayak. Kayaking tours usually start in Molyvos or Skala Kallonis and allow you to paddle along the calm waters to find secret coves and beaches. Swimming and snorkeling are frequent features of guided tours, making them excellent options for a day on the water.

Ecotourism and Wildlife Experiences

Lesvos offers many of chances for ecotourism and animal encounters because of its varied habitats, which range from lush forests and mountains to marshes and beaches. The island is a great place to visit for anyone who are interested in ecology and animals because of its dedication to maintaining its natural beauty.

Observing birds

1. Salt Pans for Kalloni

One of the greatest places in Europe to go birding is the Kalloni Salt Pans. A major resting place for migrating birds, such as several types of herons, flamingos, and raptors, is this wetland region. Birdwatchers from all over the globe come to the salt pans, especially during the spring and fall migration seasons. There are birdwatching trips available, often guided by knowledgeable locals who may share their knowledge of the many species that call the region home.

2. Kalloni Valley and Mount Olympus

There's also great birding surrounding Mount Olympus and Kalloni Valley because of their varied ecosystems. Hikers and nature lovers may view a variety of birds, including the uncommon Dalmatian pelican and different songbirds. Guided birding trips are provided, allowing an opportunity to explore the island's rich avifauna.

Nature Walks & Eco-Tours

1. Botanical Tours

Lesvos is recognized for its diverse flora, including numerous indigenous plant species. Visitors may discover more about the island's distinctive flora, including as wild herbs, medicinal plants, and the recognizable olive trees, by participating in botanical excursions guided by knowledgeable locals. These excursions often take participants through breathtaking scenery, emphasizing the richness of the island's ecological value.

2. Tours of Olive Groves

Visitors may learn about the centuries-old traditional ways of producing olive oil on the island by taking guided tours of the olive orchards. Explore the trees, sample the olive oils produced locally, and learn about the industry's significance to the island's economy and culture.

3. Tours for Nature Photography

Lesvos provides exceptional chances for photographers to capture breathtaking scenery and fauna. There are accessible guided photography trips, most of which are run by seasoned photographers who may provide advice on how to capture the island's unspoiled beauty. In order to provide a wide variety of photography subjects, these trips usually include visits to picturesque overlooks, animal areas, and traditional villages.

Preservation Activities

Numerous groups devoted to protecting the environment and conserving animals may be found on Lesvos. Through volunteer programs, educational seminars, and guided tours that showcase current conservation initiatives, visitors may interact with these organizations. By taking part in such events, visitors may enhance their awareness of the local ecosystem while also helping to preserve the island's natural heritage.

In summary

Lesvos provides a wide range of outdoor experiences and activities, from sailing and participating in water sports in its pristine seas to hiking and cycling through its stunning landscapes.

Because of the island's dedication to ecotourism and wildlife preservation, tourists may engage with the natural world while also promoting sustainable practices. Lesvos is a haven for outdoor enthusiasts seeking adventure and scenic beauty, whether they're biring in its many wetlands, sailing along the coast, or hiking through its rough trails.

CHAPTER NINE: CULTURE AND FESTIVALS IN LESVOS

Lesvos is recognized for its rich cultural history, vivid festivals, and deep-rooted customs. Throughout the year, the island organizes a variety of festivals that represent its distinct history and local traditions. Music, dancing, and creative expressions are vital to the lives of the island's people, merging historic traditions with modern influences. Visitors to Lesvos may witness a strongly rooted cultural identity that is celebrated in its festivals, music, dance, art, and local handicrafts.

Lesvos's Vibrant Festivals and Celebrations

The island's festivals represent both religious and secular traditions, offering a glimpse into the residents' way of life. Lesvos is recognized for its numerous festivities that vary from religious feasts to cultural and gastronomy festivals.

Religious Festivals

1. The Feast of Saint Raphael

One of the most prominent religious holidays in Lesvos is the Feast of Saint Raphael, observed on the Tuesday following Easter. The monastery of Saint Raphael, situated near Thermi, attracts hundreds of visitors from throughout Greece who come to venerate the saint. The celebration involves religious services, processions, and a massive assembly of the devout. Pilgrims regularly trek to the monastery from different sections of the island, performing vows and giving prayers. The festival is a very spiritual occasion that underlines the religious commitment of the islanders.

2. The Feast of the Assumption of the Virgin Mary (Panagia)

Lesvos is among the Greek islands that observe the Feast of the Assumption of the Virgin Mary on

August 15. Thousands of people congregate in the town of Agiasos to venerate the Virgin Mary, which serves as the center of these ceremonies. Religious processions center on the Panagia Agiasos church, where both residents and tourists participate in serious prayers and celebrations. Agiasos' streets come alive with the sounds of music, food vendors, and customary acts that fuse local cultural manifestations with religious solemnity.

3. The Saint Therapon Festival

Every year on May 14, the island's patron saint, Saint Therapon, is honored with a feast in Mytilene, the capital of Lesvos. Religious processions are held around the city as part of the celebration, which ends with a sizable assembly at the Church of Saint Therapon. The festival is an important cultural occasion that reflects the islanders' strong religious ties and spiritual closeness.

Cultural and culinary events

1. The Festival of Ouzo

Lesvos is well-known for producing ouzo, the well-known anise-flavored spirit from Greece. The island's most well-known product is celebrated annually in July with the Ouzo Festival. The event is often held at Plomari, the island's center of ouzo manufacturing. Tastes of many ouzo varieties, local specialties, and the distillation process are available to visitors. The festival is a lively cultural event that also features dance, music, and culinary events.

2. The Sardine Festival

Every summer, Kalloni hosts the Sardine Festival, another culinary event in Lesvos. This area is well-known for its superior sardines, and the celebration honors the community's fishing sector. Fresh grilled sardines are served to guests along with ouzo and live music. The festival is a colorful event, exhibiting the island's culinary history and offering a chance to enjoy traditional Greek hospitality.

3. The Festival of Olives

Agia Paraskevi hosts the Olive Festival to celebrate the production of olive oil, which has long been essential to the island's economy. This festival commemorates the harvest of olives, and visitors may indulge in tastings of olive oil and other olive-based goods. The event involves folk music, traditional dancing, and displays of antique olive pressing processes. It's a great chance to sample local goods and discover more about Lesvos' agricultural past.

Music, Dance, and Local Traditions

At the center of Lesvos's cultural life are music and dance, which are integral to the island's festivals, get-togethers, and celebrations. The music and dance customs of the island have a rich historical background and are influenced by both mainland Greece and Asia Minor.

Customary Soundtracks

1. Rebetiko and Folk Music

Lesvos has a significant population of rebetiko, also known as the "Greek blues," partly because of the island's closeness to Asia Minor and the influx of refugees in the early 20th century. Greek music, played on instruments like the bouzouki and baglama, conveys the joys, sorrows, and struggles of the people. Lesvos's cultural identity is largely shaped by traditional folk music in addition to Rebetiko. Folk music frequently serves as the background music for festivals, marriages, and religious ceremonies, giving islanders a soundtrack to their lives.

2. Regional Musical Instruments

The traditional musical instruments used in Lesvos reflect the island's deep cultural roots. The oud, clarinet, violin, and laouto (a type of lute) are commonly played during festivals and social gatherings. These instruments create a distinct musical sound that defines the island's folk music tradition. Visitors to Lesvos can experience live performances of traditional music at many festivals, tavernas, and local gatherings.

Dance Traditions

Dance is an essential aspect of life in Lesvos, particularly during festivals and celebrations. Traditional dances from the island include the syrtos, kalamatianos, and zeibekiko, each with its own unique rhythm and steps.

1. Syrtos

The syrto is a popular group dance performed at weddings and festivals. Dancers hold hands and move in a circular pattern, following a steady rhythm. This dance symbolizes unity and is often accompanied by live folk music.

2. Kalamatianos

Similar to the syrtos, the kalamatianos is another group dance performed at social gatherings. It is one of the most recognizable dances in Greece, with its lively steps and energetic pace. Dancers form a large circle, and the lead dancer often improvises movements, adding a creative flair to the performance.

3. Zeibekiko

The zeibekiko is a solo dance that expresses deep emotion and personal reflection. It is often performed to Rebetiko music and features slow, deliberate movements. The zeibekiko is a dance of individual expression and is considered one of the most profound and symbolic dances in Greek culture.

Art and Handicrafts in Lesvos

Lesvos has a long tradition of craftsmanship, with local artisans producing beautiful works of art and crafts. Visitors can explore workshops and local markets to discover handmade items that reflect the island's cultural and artistic heritage.

Pottery and ceramics

Pottery has been practiced in Lesvos for centuries, and the island is known for its high-quality ceramics. The village of Mantamados is famous for its pottery workshops, where visitors can see artisans at work, creating traditional terra-cotta pots and decorative items. Mantamados pottery is often adorned with intricate patterns and designs inspired by the island's natural beauty and ancient traditions. Visitors can purchase unique, handmade pieces as souvenirs or gifts.

Weaving and embroidery

Traditional weaving and embroidery are also significant aspects of Lesvos's artistic culture. Women in rural villages have passed down these skills through generations, creating intricate textiles used in clothing, household items, and religious ceremonies. The village of Agiasos is known for its handwoven textiles and embroidered items, which are often made using natural materials such as wool and cotton. These items are highly valued for their craftsmanship and beauty, reflecting the island's cultural identity.

Wood Carving

Wood carving is another ancient trade in Lesvos, with artists crafting elaborate works that vary from religious icons to ornamental things. The community of Agiasos is famous for its excellent woodworkers who make beautiful carvings, frequently influenced by Byzantine art and religious themes. Visitors may tour workshops where craftsmen continue to practice this historic technique, preserving the island's creative legacy.

Painting and Contemporary Art

Lesvos has also become a hotspot for modern art, with some local artists and foreign artists making the island their home. Mytilene features various art galleries and shows that present a combination of traditional and contemporary creative expressions. The island's natural beauty, lively culture, and historical importance inspire many artists, resulting in a rich and diversified creative landscape.

In summary

Lesvos's culture is a dynamic tapestry woven from its rich history, religious traditions, music, dance, and creative manifestations. The island's festivals are a cheerful celebration of life, allowing tourists a unique chance to explore local customs and traditions. Whether it's the sound of folk music, the sight of dancers in traditional costumes, or the workmanship of local craftsmen, Lesvos's cultural legacy is profoundly entwined with its everyday existence. Through its festivals, music, dancing, and art, Lesvos presents an extraordinary cultural trip that portrays the character and soul of the island.

CHAPTER TEN: CONCLUSION: PLANNING YOUR PERFECT LESVOS GETAWAY

There are a few essential elements to consider when organizing your ideal Lesvos vacation for 2024–2025 in order to make it enjoyable and well-planned. Making the most of your time on this stunning Greek island will depend on a number of factors, including when to visit, important travel advice, and useful suggestions. When planning the perfect Lesvos vacation, every detail counts, from knowing the best months to go to helpful advice on lodging, transportation, and dining.

When to Visit Lesvos in 2024-2025

Lesvos has hot, dry summers and moderate winters due to its Mediterranean environment. Whatever type of experience you're looking for, the island's varied attractions and scenery make it attractive all year round.

Summertime Peak (June–August)

The busiest travel seasons for tourists visiting Lesvos are June through August. The weather is at its hottest, with average highs of 28°C (82°F) to 35°C (95°F), and the island is teeming with visitors during this time. The liveliest beaches are Vatera and Skala Eressos, where social gatherings, water sports, and beach bars are all in full swing. There are also many festivals and cultural events, which provide a great way to learn about and participate in regional customs and festivities.

Peak season, however, can mean more expensive lodging and congested conditions in some areas, particularly in and around popular tourist destinations like Mytilene and Molyvos. It's crucial to reserve lodging and travel well in advance if you intend to visit during this time.

April-May and September-October are shoulder seasons.

The shoulder season, which runs from September to October and April to May, is often cited as the ideal time to go to Lesvos. During these months, the weather stays comfortable, with temperatures ranging from 20°C (68°F) to 27°C (81°F), making it excellent for experiencing the island's natural beauty, trekking, and touring without the strong summer heat. Beaches are quieter, but the water is still warm enough for swimming.

This season is also perfect for seeing Lesvos's cultural and historical landmarks like the Mytilene Castle or Petrified Forest, with fewer people and more relaxed circumstances. If you appreciate birding, Kalloni Salt Pans are most busy during the migratory seasons of spring and fall.

Winter Season (December to March)

While November to March represents the low season on Lesvos, it's still worth considering if you're interested in a tranquil, off-the-beaten-path vacation. The winter months are warm, with temperatures between 10°C (50°F) and 15°C (59°F), while rain is more common. This is the time to experience a calmer island, great for people interested in cultural immersion, seeing historic villages, and soaking up the slower pace of life.

Many businesses, including hotels and restaurants, may shut during the off-season, particularly in smaller settlements, although you may still find lodgings in Mytilene and Molyvos. Winter is also an excellent season to experience the island's famed hot springs at Eftalou or Polichnitos, giving a peaceful escape.

Must-Know Travel Tips and Recommendations

Here are some crucial pointers and suggestions to make sure your vacation to Lesvos goes well and improves your experience:

Accommodations: Lesvos has a range of lodging choices, including self-catering flats, charming guesthouses, and opulent hotels. It's best to make reservations well in advance during peak season, particularly if you're staying in well-known locations like Mytilene, Petra, or Skala Eressos. For a more genuine experience, try staying in a historic village like Agiasos or Plomari, where you may appreciate local hospitality and a slower pace of life.

Vatera Beach offers a variety of beachside lodging alternatives, from low-cost hostels to mid-range hotels, if that's your preference. Excellent coastal hotels and guesthouses with breathtaking views of the Aegean Sea can also be found at Molyvos and Petra.

Moving

Lesvos is quite simple to navigate, but if you want the flexibility to see the island's more isolated spots, renting a vehicle is the best choice. Lesvos has a well-kept road system that makes it possible to go to lesser-known destinations like the Petrified Forest and the sleepy interior settlements.

Buses linking large towns like Mytilene, Kalloni, and Molyvos are a common means of transit for individuals who prefer public transport. But bus service to more remote locations may be scarce, so if you depend on public transportation, making plans in advance is crucial.

Although they are an option, taxi fares might be higher, especially for longer trips. It's a good idea to settle on the fee before you leave if you want to take a cab.

Eating and Cooking

Lesvos is well known for its cuisine, especially its ouzo, olive oil, and fresh fish. Must-try regional delicacies include kefte (meatballs), gigantic beans in tomato sauce, and sardeles pastes (salted sardines). The seaside villages of Plomari and Skala Kallonis are well-known for their top-notch fish tavernas, where you may savor the day's fresh catch.

Around the island, there are a lot of eateries and pubs serving regional cuisine prepared using products from neighboring farms and the surrounding waters. Excellent eating choices, ranging from informal cafes to more upmarket businesses, can also be found in Agiasos and Mytilene. Enjoy some of the regional delicacies, such as amigdalota (almond biscuits) and the classic Greek pastries made with walnuts and honey.

Pick up fresh vegetables, bread, and regional cheeses at one of the island's numerous markets, including the Mytilene Municipal Market, if you're staying in self-catering lodging. For foodies wishing to sample the diverse cuisine of Lesvos, these markets give a genuine glimpse of local life.

Local Customs and Etiquette

Greece is renowned for its warm friendliness, and Lesvos is no exception. Although the people are kind and inviting, it's important to observe certain customs:

When visiting monasteries or churches, wear modest clothing.

It's traditional to send a modest gift, like flowers or candies, if you're welcomed to someone's house. Tipping is customary but not required at restaurants. If you get excellent service, it's appreciated if you leave around 5–10% of the cost.

Safety and Health

Lesvos has a low crime rate, making it a safe vacation destination. But, much as at any other vacation, it's crucial to watch out for your possessions, particularly in busy places and during festivals.

There are medical facilities on the island, like health clinics in major towns and hospitals in Mytilene. Bring extra medicine with you if you need it for the duration of your trip, since access to pharmacies may be restricted in certain remote locations.

Although bottled water is more readily accessible and often preferred by the locals, tap water is typically safe to consume.

Essentials for Packing

Depending on the season, take into account the following packing advice while visiting Lesvos:

To protect yourself from the intense Mediterranean heat in the summer, bring lots of sunscreen, a hat, sunglasses, and light, breathable clothes.

Bring layers and a waterproof jacket if you're going during the colder months, since rain is likely to fall.

Comfortable walking shoes are a must for exploring the island's picturesque paths, olive orchards, and historical monuments.

If you want to take advantage of the stunning beaches or hot springs in Lesvos, don't forget to pack swimsuits.

Final Thoughts and Farewell

Lesvos is a place that caters to all kinds of tourists, including those who like the beach, history, cuisine, and the outdoors. Its unique combination of breathtaking scenery, friendly hospitality, and cultural history guarantees that guests will have an enriching and unforgettable vacation.

Lesvos has a certain allure that enthralls everyone who visits, whether they go in the quiet off-season or the busy summer months. The variety of the island is absolutely amazing, ranging from the historic remains of Mytilene to the tranquil olive fields and birding locations of Kalloni. Remember these crucial pointers and advice when you organize the ideal vacation to Lesvos in 2024–2025 to guarantee a seamless, pleasurable, and memorable experience.

In the end, Lesvos is a location to really experience, not merely a place to visit, leaving travelers with priceless memories and a need to come back. Happy exploring!

SAFE JOURNEYS!!!

Printed in Dunstable, United Kingdom

66777431R00067